Live from the Beginning of Time

Late Night Comedy Monologues Through the Ages

Ben Alper

ISBN- 979-8-218-38906-2

Cover and book design by David Lennon

First Printing edition

Right Side Publications

www.bennettalper.com

Bennett.Alper@gmail.com

For my family

Table of Contents

Introduction

Welcome to the book. What a great group of readers we have tonight!

Late-night talk shows entertain, inform and remind us when the president mispronounces Azerbaijan.

Late-night hosts are modern-day town criers who play it strictly for laughs. Without them, we'd never know the presidents' positions on foreign relations, or their relations with foreign floozies named Fiona.

From Steve Allen in the 1950s to Stephen Colbert today, the highlight of late-night TV shows is the opening monologue. It's hard to imagine a time when there wasn't a Steve, Jack, Johnny, Dave, Jay, Stephen, Jimmy or Jimmy observing politics and celebrity indiscretions, particularly ones that include the words "arrested," "Clinton," "rehab" and "Trump."

All of this made me wonder: What if throughout history there had been late-night talk show hosts performing nightly monologues?

What if a host offered his take on Hannibal haggling with a used elephant salesman? Or wondered if Mrs. Ben Franklin ever said, "Fix your own dinner, Mister Founding Father!"

This book answers these questions and more.

How? Historians can only rely on thoroughly researched facts. Comedy writers have additional access to rumors, innuendo, hearsay and a twisted imagination.

Will you learn something by reading these historical comedy monologues? It depends on whether you attended an elite educational institution or dozed through Zoom University.

I guarantee, however, after reading *Live From the Beginning of Time*, you will never be stumped if someone asks, "Was Joan of Arc partial to a dry heat?"

You've been a great reader so far. I hope you stick around for the rest of the book.

Ben Alper

Chapter 1:
Let's See What's
Happening in the
World.

2,000,000 BC
Homo Erectus Walks on Two Legs

- New inhabitants have been spotted in the neighborhood who walk on only two legs. They use the other two limbs for gesturing, "Look at me! I can walk on two feet!"

- They call their former front legs "arms." I call them lazy limbs that let the other two legs do the walking.

- It makes no sense. Who needs arms when you can push things with your nose?

- The two-legged, upright snobs are always looking down on us, not that they have a choice.

- They use their arms for something called hugging—or as the males call it, getting to first rock.

- Guys, we're in trouble. Women are starting to complain, "Four legs are nice, but there's something about a tall man with two arms."

- The ladies are also attracted to their sloped foreheads and hairless bodies. Say goodbye to the days when they longed to be held in your four strong legs.

- Their dual-legged leader will be on the show tomorrow for his first face-to-knee interview.

1,000,000 BC
Fire Discovered by Humans

- There's a new thing called fire. Or as many people are calling it, "Ouch! What is that?"

- It's amazing what you can do with fire—like burn to death.

- Fire is hard to describe—particularly since we have a vocabulary of only three words and five grunts.

- As far as we know, it was discovered when a guy rubbed two sticks together, which made them really hot—after which his wife said, "Why can't you rub me like that?"

- Of course, now we need to come up with a God of Fire. However, the God of Water says his brother is available.

- It's also fun to sit around a fire and tell spooky stories—especially stories that end with someone yelling, "Help, I'm on fire!"

- But the greatest thing about fire is we can now tell our "It's so hot" jokes.

41,000 BC
German Erotic Cave Art

- An artist named Shlomo Sapien has created some erotic etchings on his cave walls. We don't know who modeled for him, but they are certainly frisky.

- The couple on the cave wall look like they're having more fun than a wolf that just learned to lick itself.

- Some of the stone carvings in this artist's cave resemble male and female private parts. In fact, this is the only cave that gets aroused if you wink and blow it a kiss.

- Shlomo says his work is actually all about fertility rituals. You'd be pretty fertile too if your ritual was sculpting naked people's naughty parts.

- These may be the first fertility rituals that have a two-drink minimum.

- One of our writers was asked to model for the artist. Unfortunately, he had trouble maintaining his stone formation.

- Some people miss the old fertility rituals—where you asked a girl's parents for permission to drag her away by her hair.

- The good news is the fertility ritual seems to be working. The bad news is every baby born so far looks like a guy in the village named Ogling Org.

4500 BC
Invention of the Wheel

- Did you hear about this guy, Grog, who invented something called the wheel? Although, pardon me, he now insists on being called Grog the Inventor.

- It's a round wooden disk he claims will make life more bearable. That's nice, but can we first find a way to stop people from whining about being eaten alive by wild animals?

- They say the wheel could advance civilization. Call me old-fashioned, but what's wrong with carrying heavy loads on your back until you collapse?

- And you know the minute Grog told his girlfriend he'd invented the wheel, she said, "Big deal, Loana's boyfriend invented the bow and arrow."

- The "experts" say the wheel works best in pairs. Of course they do. Inventors are always trying to sell you something extra.

- If you're thinking about buying a used wheel, be careful about any salesman who says it was owned by a little old lady who only pushed it to scare evil spirits on Sundays.

- We hope you enjoy the rest of the show, if we're not attacked by a neighboring tribe.

From the Desk

5 Interesting Facts About New Invention Beer

- Finally, something useful to do with wheat and barley.

- After a few drinks, it's hard to pronounce "fermentation."

- After a few more drinks, you forget which orifice the beer is supposed to go in.

- The God of Beer is the first deity with a beer belly.

- ... and the second deity that belches.

2700 BC
Creation of the Abacus

- There's a new tool called the abacus. It takes the place of counting with your fingers and toes—which means you'll need a new excuse when someone asks, "Why are you playing with yourself?"

- The abacus is a flat board with pebbles you move around to add, subtract, multiply and divide. It's extremely accurate unless your crooked business partner is cooking the abacus.

- The abacus is a very versatile instrument. Kids love using it to count large numbers, and old-timers love using it to pound their pomegranate seeds.

- It's totally changing the way we work. In the time it takes to calculate something by scratching marks in the ground, you can hand the abacus to someone and say, "You figure it out."

- Our show's ticket takers find the abacus helpful for calculating how many apples to return in exchange for a radish and an ear of corn.

- Of course, you know the minute you finally break down and buy an abacus, they'll be charging you double for the new version with magic pebbles.

- I guess we shouldn't be skeptical of progress. Remember when we thought our show's first host was crazy because he stopped drawing his jokes on a cave wall?

2490 BC
Building of the Great Pyramid of Giza

- They finally finished the Great Pyramid of Giza. Most people were pleasantly surprised. They were expecting the Fair-to-Middling Pyramid of Giza.

- I like this pyramid even though, truth be told, I've always been a sphere guy.

- The Great Pyramid was built as a tomb for Pharaoh Khufu. I hope, wherever he is, he's happy with it and not thinking, "Dammit, I should've requested more leg room."

- It's the tallest man-made structure in the world. Although, when the builders of the Sphinx heard about it, they quickly announced plans to give their monument taller cat ears.

- To build the pyramid, workers quarried an estimated 2.3 million gigantic blocks weighing six million tons total, which comes to approximately 1.5 hernias per block.

- And contrary to what people are saying, slave labor was not used to build the pyramid. Everyone was paid—at least according to the Brotherhood of Indentured Servants Union.

- Some of the workers are with us tonight. Please stand up if you can.

2000 BC
Stonehenge Completed

- We're coming to you this week from the newly completed Stonehenge. It took about 1,500 years to build—seven without the lunch and water breaks.

- Let's have a shoutout to the workers here tonight. They're the ones wearing little animal skins that read, "I destroyed my back building Stonehenge and all I got was this lousy loin cloth."

- I see lots of celebrities in the audience—many who managed to reach their seats without being attacked by wild hedgehogs.

- Stonehenge is made up of 100 giant upright stones placed in a circular layout. Why? Because if you buy ninety-nine, the hundredth is free.

- How big are these stones? One engineer was attacked by laborers for continually saying, "Move it to the left ... a little to the right ... no, move it back ..."

- Some claim Stonehenge is the handiwork of the wizard Merlin. That explains why he's here tonight selling his overpriced potions.

- We'll be right back after this brief pagan sacrifice from our sponsor.

1755 BC
Code of Hammurabi is Issued

- King Hammurabi has written an extensive set of laws to govern us. Amazingly, it lists no penalties for spouses who snore.

- The Code was carved onto a massive, finger-shaped black stone pillar. So far, only one legal scholar has been able to read it without throwing out his neck.

- The Code lists 282 laws—so many that Hammurabi had to come up with new crimes like illicit winking at fertility goddesses.

- One law says, "If a man put out the eye of another man, his eye shall be put out." If it's a third offense, a belly button will suffice.

- Another edict is, "If a man steals an ox, then he must pay back thirty times its value." You can bet some guy who gets the penalties mixed up will get trampled trying to put out the ox's eye.

- Hammurabi's Code also says an accused person is considered innocent until proven guilty. The legal translation? You've got more time to come up with an alibi.

- Our show is adjusting to the new Code. From now on, we will no longer whip our writers until *after* their jokes fail to get laughs.

508 BC
Athens Introduces Democracy

- Athens has a new system of self-rule called democracy—which basically means if you don't like how your government is being run, you can complain to yourself.

- The term democracy means "rule by the people." And what people better to govern than your crazy neighbor who thinks he's a goat.

- Things are changing already. Today, I saw a sad fellow holding a sign that read, "Out of work tyrant will heartlessly rule for food."

- Under democracy, people can replace their government through peaceful transfer of power rather than violent uprising or revolution. The last time anybody passed anything on to me peacefully was when I slept with a woman named Limber Luna.

- All adult male citizens will be required to take an active part in the new democratic government. If they don't, they'll be fined and marked with red paint—which will make their wives even angrier for clashing with the curtains.

- We decided to run our show like a democracy. If I don't get enough laughs tonight, tomorrow we vote on which writer gets thrown to the lions.

1200 BC

5 Comments Overheard Inside the Trojan Horse

- I requested a window seat.

- I would've gone with a big wooden turtle.

- Your bench cushion can be used as a battering device.

- It's not a birthday party. Don't yell "Surprise!"

- Are we there yet?

400 BC
Vātsyāyana Writes the Kama Sutra

- A man named Vātsyāyana has written a book about sexuality called the Kama Sutra. It's so hot, my assistant spent the entire week underlining the good parts.

- In honor of Mr. Vātsyāyana's presence tonight, we've changed the Applause sign to "Fondle and Caress."

- He was actually going to be on another show this evening but their host said, "Not tonight, I'm just not in the mood."

- Vātsyāyana says there are sixty-three positions for great sex. Sixty-four if you count bent over catching your breath.

- The Kama Sutra is also about the philosophy and theory of love—and how to untangle yourself after attempting positions thirty-seven through forty-eight.

- We talk to people with all kinds of positions on this show, but not two thighs wrapped around your neck.

- However, Vātsyāyana doesn't explain the most important position, diving out a window while escaping your lover's spouse.

- I guarantee, after tonight's show, you'll be asking, "Was the interview good for you?"

323 BC
Alexander the Great Dies

- Now that Alexander III of Macedon has died, people are referring to him as Alexander the Great. A little late. I mean, wouldn't you want people calling you "The Pretty Damn Good" while you were alive?

- The least they could've done while he was alive was present him with a "Way to Conquer!" plaque.

- Alexander was king of Macedonia and Persia, ruler of the Greeks, and when he was alive, we didn't even think of calling him Alexander the Wowza!!!

- Did I mention he was also an Egyptian pharaoh? I've been more complimentary to my slave who's also my press agent.

- Even as a teenager, his tutor Aristotle called him Alexander the Could Be Greater If He Applied Himself.

- The fact he named many cities after himself including Alexandria in Egypt was obviously nothing more than a cry for help.

- So, better late than never. Here's my tribute to Alexander III of Macedon. He was so great he could destroy the Persian Empire while riding sidesaddle.

71 BC
Spartacus Leads Slave Revolt

- Spartacus the Thracian gladiator is leading a slave revolt against the Romans. Put simply, this is a one-man terror in a tunic.

- He originally served in a Roman auxiliary unit, deserted, and became an insurgent against the Romans—which led to him being disinvited to the Roman Auxiliary Unit reunion.

- Later, Spartacus was captured, brought to Rome and sold as a slave—but his new owner only agreed to buy him after being offered 1.4% APR financing.

- While a slave, he was enrolled in his master's gladiator school and, like all the other slaves, on full scholarship.

- Spartacus helped organize a breakout leading to more than seventy gladiator slaves escaping, using improvised weapons they got from the kitchen. That's where he got his first nickname, Spartacus the Melon Baller.

- Spartacus and his co-leaders raided supplies, then began attacking the Republic's military, who initially were confused by a gladiator waving a melon baller.

- We were thinking about having Spartacus make a special appearance tonight, but we were afraid he'd misunderstand the difference between a surprise guest and a surprise attack.

7 BC
Dentures Invented

- A man in Etruria has invented false teeth. It's the perfect gift for anyone tired of gumming "I love you."

- The dentures are made of actual human and animal teeth. You can tell if you've got the animal teeth, because they're a little worn down from chewing on people.

- Also, if you smile at a wolf, it may think you're flirting.

- But I'd go with the animal teeth if you like that snarly, bloodthirsty look.

- The fake teeth are fastened together with gold bands—which instantly makes your mouth richer than you'll ever be.

- Dentures give you a nice smile—or a grimace if you wear them upside down.

- Having a full set of teeth is a real status symbol. For example, only people with teeth can pronounce the phrase "status symbol."

From the Desk

41 AD

Emperor Caligula's Orgy
Dos and Don'ts

- Do BYOBF (Bring Your Own Bodily Fluids).

- Don't roll in the free buffet while engaging in threesomes.

- Do firmly attach your name tag before hanging upside down by your testicles.

- Don't network while mounting a potential business opportunity.

- Do introduce yourself while flogging strangers.

- Don't forget to tip the one-eyed eunuch.

80 AD
Roman Colosseum Completed

- Construction on the new Colosseum in Rome has been completed. You should check it out while it still has that new amphitheater smell.

- Finally, a great place to take your family and kids to watch some nice, wholesome gladiator fights.

- Construction began under Emperor Vespasian—or as he's now known, Emperor Kickback.

- The Colosseum can hold an estimated 50,000 to 80,000 people—30,000 of those being slaves serving as cushioned seats.

- Actually, the Colosseum was built by 100,000 slaves—which probably explains why they went overboard with the "Bond Servant Refreshment and Orgy Lounge."

- I'm not saying our show can compare with the entertainment they'll have at the Colosseum, but only on our program can you watch two guests fight to their death while engaging in witty repartee.

- It's my dream that one day people will think about me and say, "He killed at the Colosseum."

Creation of the Hippocratic Oath

- A Greek doctor named Hippocrates has created an oath of medical ethics. I hope this pledge also says something about never sticking your hand under a patient's robe to grab their money sack.

- Actually, a medical ethics oath is a great idea. Who among us hasn't staggered out of our doctor's office wondering, "Did I really need the Babylonian Skull Cure?"

- Hippocrates' oath includes, "I swear by Apollo Healer, by Asclepius, by Hygieia, by Panacea, and by all the gods and goddesses..." That's quite a group practice he's got.

- Coincidentally, Hippocrates neglects to mention the most important medical deity, Thiefius, the god of Highway Robbery.

- I'd be happy if my doctor pledged not to charge me an arm and a leg for removing an arm and a leg.

- The most important part of Hippocrates' medical oath is "First, do no harm." Frankly, I wish he'd started with "First, wash your hands."

- It's also inspired me to create my own oath: First, tell no unfunny joke. Second, if I do, have the guy who wrote it examined by an angry tiger.

376 AD
Fall of the Western Roman Empire

- The big story this week has been the fall of the Roman Empire—and, of course, Spring Toga Fashion Month.

- Because of the fall, there's no stability in the government. How bad is it? Three of my writers are deposed emperors, and another is a laid-off gladiator.

- Two more now spend most of their time at Circus Maximus betting on the chariots.

- A lot of people are blaming the Empire's fall on moral decay, although there are no complaints from our proud sponsor, Tiberius' Discount Orgies.

- The fall of the Empire is affecting everyone. When he heard the news, the eunuch who cleans my office asked, "Does this mean I can get my testicles back?"

- You didn't hear it from me, but things were never the same after we were invaded by Attila the Hun. Nothing personal, but never trust anyone who's name ends with "the Hun"—or begins with "Barbarian King."

- Whoaa, I can see we have some barbarians in the audience. Don't be so sensitive. My sister-in-law is a barbarian. My brother met her at a "Let's Pillage a Village" mixer.

600 AD
Pope Gregory I Compiles the Seven Deadly Sins

- Pope Gregory has compiled what he calls the Seven Deadly Sins. That's nice, but would it be asking too much to have just one feel-good-about-yourself sin?

- The Seven Deadly Sins are pride, envy, anger, sloth, greed, gluttony, and lust—or as my wife calls them, me on my best behavior.

- This has definitely hurt business at the new eatery down the street, "Glutton's All-You-Can-Vomit Buffet."

- You don't want to mix the sins up. One of our writers was dumped by a girlfriend after he told her, "I sloth for you."

- Pope Gregory analyzed the cardinal sins in his authoritative text Moralia and trimmed their number to seven. How'd you like to be the one who had to tell Apathy it was too lazy to make the cut?

- Pope Gregory says the Seven Deadly Sins are those transgressions that are fatal to spiritual progress. On the plus side, Annoying is breathing a sigh of relief.

- Are these sins really deadly? I mean, have you ever heard a doctor say, "We did our best to save him, but he was just too envious."

From the Desk

1087 AD

5 William the Conqueror Nicknames That Didn't Stick

- William the Slightly More Than Disconcerted

- William the Don't Get Me Started

- William the Are You Talking to Me?

- William the Not the Kind of Conqueror You Want to Mess With

- William That's Conqueror with a Capital C

1095 AD
Crusades Begin

- The Crusades began this week—which means there's never been a better time to sublet a hovel from anyone flying a "Jerusalem or Bust" flag on their door.

- I was thinking of going, but I'm allergic to being impaled in a sword fight.

- This whole thing started when Pope Urban II proclaimed the First Crusade at the Council of Clermont—which was surprising, since many ecclesiastics and laymen just came for the free buffet.

- Most Crusaders are peasants with no combat experience. In fact, their first training lesson was identifying the pointy end of their spear.

- No one is more in favor of reclaiming the Holy Land in the Middle East for Christianity than me. In fact, "Can I offer you religious salvation?" is my best pickup line.

- Almost all of our writers have joined the Crusades. We're down to three heretical Christians and a one-legged pagan.

- But even though our last few writers aren't believers, if we get laughs tonight, we've promised them absolution from purgatory in the afterlife.

1100 AD
Sir Lancelot Will Not Be On the Show

- I feel like an idiot. All week I've been hounding the staff to get Sir Lancelot on the show; and my producer kept saying, "He doesn't exist." I said, "That's what you said about Merlin the Wizard I hired for my kid's birthday party."

- I even offered our booking agent a five-pig knuckle bonus if he could get Lancelot on our show—and I normally never pay him more than three pig knuckles.

- Guess what? They were right. He's a fictional character, and I feel like an idiot. This is more embarrassing than when we booked the guest who claimed he'd invented a catapult that could heave a family of six to Spain.

- It also explains why King Arthur, Queen Guinevere and Sir Galahad have yet to return my messages—and why they won't be joining our round table discussion.

- I'm disappointed. I really wanted to ask Lancelot about the stories of him slaying dragons and giants. Were they true or was it just the ale talking?

- Fortunately, we have an excellent guest who will be filling in for Lancelot tonight. She's written an interesting and informative book called "I Was Married to Robin Hood's Merriest Man."

1300 AD
Marco Polo Returns from Asia

- Marco Polo has returned to Venice after twenty-four years of traveling through Asia along the Silk Road. Amazingly, his cat was still sitting in the window ignoring him.

- Marco Polo comes from a family of world travelers. In fact, they were the first people to coin the term "group discount."

- He's one of the first Europeans to explore the vast Orient, which includes many peoples and cultures. He's also one of the first persons to ask in multiple languages, "Can you point me to your restroom?"

- Actually, Marco's father and uncle first journeyed to Asia before him. He decided to go there himself after his dad brought him back a silk housecoat embroidered with, "Danger, Family Vacation In Progress."

- Polo arrived in China at age twenty and served for seventeen years as Chinese Emperor Kublai Khan's foreign emissary—a job that mostly involved telling foreign dignitaries, "I don't know what he's saying either."

- Marco's account of his travels through the Orient contains the first references to paper money. It's described in a chapter titled "Oops, I Thought It Was Toilet Paper."

- Marco will be on the show next week to plug his hilarious new book, *101 Mongolian Herdsman Jokes.*

Chapter 2:
What Else Is
Happening in the
World?

1455 AD
Gutenberg Invents the Printing Press

- A guy named Johannes Gutenberg has designed and built the first mechanized printing press in Europe. It's a real timesaver for anyone who writes lots of ransom notes.

- He's using it to print his "Gutenberg Bible." It's like most Bibles except he's changed "God" to "Almighty Gutenberg."

- Gutenberg's printing press is expected to quicken the spread of knowledge, discoveries, and literacy—or at the very least, fill our homes with unread books that make us appear smart.

- Everything is being printed on it now. In fact, halfway through the last joke we received a printed legal notice asking "You call this comedy?"

- Just one of Gutenberg's movable-type printing presses can produce up to 3,600 pages per workday—triple that if you lubricate it with double espresso.

- And if you're a dirty old man, now you can easily send obscene notes that include a dedication, introduction and table of contents.

- Thankfully, we ordered one of Gutenberg's printing presses for our crazy cue card guy, "Scribbling" Sebastiano. The only problem is now he writes the jokes in Latin.

From the Desk

1346 AD

5 Signs You May Have the Bubonic Plague

- You woke up spooning a cuddly rat.

- You think of diarrhea, nausea and vomiting as the good old days.

- Your wife is introducing the children to their "new dad."

- Your birthday cake says "Bubonic Bertha."

- Your most recent doctor's bill listed "examination," "diagnosis" and "coffin."

1512 AD
Michelangelo Paints the Sistine Chapel Ceiling

- After four long years, Michelangelo finally finished painting a mural on the Sistine Chapel ceiling. That's four back-breaking years while constantly being asked, "Can we move the furniture back now?"

- Pope Julius II, who commissioned him to do it, took one look at the ceiling that included nine scenes from the Book of Genesis and said, "I'm so glad we didn't go with the off-white."

- For some reason the mural contains many nude male youths. So far, no explanation from Michelangelo or his assistants, young Lorenzo, young Tommaso, young Matteo or young Federico.

- Originally, the Sistine Chapel's ceiling was painted blue and covered with golden stars. Michelangelo took one look and said, "You know what you need? More nude male youths."

- Michelangelo is primarily known for his nude sculpture of David—which like his mural, continues to make people ask, "Can someone please teach this guy to sculpt a pair of pants?"

- So far, praise for Michelangelo's masterpiece has been almost universal, although there will always be those snobs who say, "You missed that spot on the left."

1543 AD
Nicolaus Copernicus' Heliocentric System Theory

- Astronomer Nicolaus Copernicus has a theory the Earth is not the center of the universe. Rather, it revolves around the Sun. When I heard that, I almost fell off the planet.

- He's pretty certain of this theory. However, not certain enough to tell his wife the world doesn't revolve around her.

- Copernicus' thesis is called the heliocentric system—as in, "What the heliocentric is Copernicus talking about?"

- He published this theory in his book *On the Revolutions of the Heavenly Spheres.* Until now, most men thought heavenly spheres belonged to women with pleasant bottoms.

- Copernicus is no slouch. He's a practicing physician, economist, diplomat, scholar and has a doctorate in canon law. When he was a student, the world's greatest minds traveled from all over Europe just to copy off his homework.

- It's hard to believe the Sun and not the Earth is the center of the solar system. That's like saying the moon is made of Gouda and not green cheese.

- Copernicus also thinks the Earth rotates daily on its axis. Even more after it's had a few drinks.

1604 AD
First English Language Dictionary Published

- A clergyman named Robert Cawdrey has created the first English language dictionary, called the *Table Alphabeticall*. Everyone should have one—or two if you talk out of both sides of your mouth.

- Now there's something new to say to our kids: "I don't know. Look it up."

- Cawdrey says he created his dictionary because the average person speaks English poorly—especially crazy people who grunt and scream in the wrong tense.

- His dictionary contains about 2,500 words—including every word that's implied after saying, "... and so on and so forth."

- Now, you can tell people trying to impress you with their large vocabulary to look up "pretentious" and "presumptuous."

- I must say, however, even though the dictionary is very comprehensive, it doesn't include half the words written on our privy wall.

- I now understand when my staff tells me, "You're an idiot," and they understand when I say, "You're fired."

1610 AD
Galileo Galilei Discovers 4 Moons Orbiting Jupiter

- Using a telescope, Galileo Galilei discovered there are four moons orbiting Jupiter. Amazing! I couldn't see the guy who hit me with a rotten tomato last week.

- Although he didn't invent the telescope, Galileo did improve the design. For example, he added a wine glass holder.

- He's also one of the first to use a telescope for something other than spying on the woman next door taking a bath.

- While stargazing, Galileo discovered the moon's surface is not smooth. Rather, it has craters, mountains and razor stubble.

- Galileo is also a prominent mathematician and a philosopher. In fact, he has so many fancy titles, he can't see the end of them even with his telescope.

- Galileo supports Copernicus' theory that the Sun is the center of the universe and the Earth and other planets revolve around it. Either that or the planets are actually bugs crawling across his telescope lens.

- Because of his theory, Galileo will have to stand trial before the Inquisition in Rome. He was last seen searching through his telescope for a good lawyer.

From the Desk

1509 AD

5 Henry VIII Tips for a Great Marriage

- Get to know your wife before beheading her.

- Nothing gets a woman in the mood like gently whispering, "Time to create a male heir."

- ... and nothing gets a woman out of the mood like having her arrested for showing interest in Protestantism.

- That "more to love" saying doesn't apply after you've passed 400 pounds.

- It's not always about you. Just kidding, it's always about you.

1687 AD
Isaac Newton Develops
3 Laws of Motion

- Isaac Newton has developed what he calls his Principia Mathematica. Sounds complicated? Not as complicated as writing jokes about something called Principia Mathematica.

- Newton is a brilliant mathematician, physicist, astronomer, alchemist, theologian and author. Our smartest writer is a guy who can balance a grape on his nose.

- Newton has developed three laws of motion. The first one is: An object will not change its motion unless a force acts on it. Meaning, if you fall down drunk, you can always count on the floor to stop you.

- Newton's second law is: The force on an object is equal to its mass times its acceleration. In other words, smart people are more likely to know why they fell on the floor.

- His third law of motion conflicts with my law: No more than two laws of motion jokes.

- Mr. Newton will be on the show next week to talk about his book *Mathematical Principles of Natural Philosophy*, and I'll be pretending to understand what on earth he's talking about.

1765 AD
First Restaurant Opens in Paris

- A new kind of eating place has opened in Paris. It's called a "restaurant." It's like an inn or tavern—only you don't have to share a table with a traveling band of Prussian acrobats.

- The front of the restaurant displays the Latin phrase, "Venite ad me omnes qui stomacho laboratis, et ego vos restaurabo," which roughly translates to, "Come to me, those whose stomachs ache, and I will empty your wallet."

- The restaurant has small round tables like in cafés. No more passing the potatoes down a long table through three neighborhoods.

- Owner Mathurin Roze de Chantoiseau claims his food is healthy and will restore your strength. In fact, it's given some customers the strength to heave him through a window after seeing their bill.

- The restaurant also has something called a "menu" that allows you to choose from a list of items—which beats the old way: eating whatever the previous customer didn't finish.

- Another great feature, unlike at inns and taverns, if you tip the owner, he won't seat you in the privy.

- Our entire staff is going to the restaurant after the show. With all the menu choices, I still haven't decided which dish to send back.

1789 AD
Storming of the Bastille Prison

- Today's storming of the Bastille Prison could be the start of the French Revolution—and the end of the jail's all-you-can-eat croissant brunch.

- The prison had become a symbol of the monarchy's dictatorial rule—despite the addition of string quartets in each solitary confinement cell.

- The crowd gathered around the Bastille at dawn, armed with muskets, swords and makeshift weapons—plus a few pacifists wielding deadly feather dusters.

- There were only seven prisoners left in the jail, not including the Marquis de Sade who'd been transferred out days earlier for complaining he wasn't being tortured enough.

- At about 1:30, the rabble stormed the prison. Their message was loud and clear, No more Monsieur Nice Mob.

- The crowd immediately screamed for prison governor de Launay's head—and his head is in our audience tonight, on a pike blocking the person seated behind him.

- A programming note: King Louis XVI and wife Marie Antoinette will not be on the show tomorrow. Instead, our guest will be famed puppeteer Gaston and his talking guillotine.

From the Desk
1510 AD

5 of Leonardo da Vinci's Lesser-Known Inventions

- Steam-powered dental floss

- Adults only anatomy book

- Automatic pie thrower

- Lambskin whoopie cushion

- Special glasses that make Mona Lisa look like she's winking

1796 AD
Catherine the Great's Rumored Demise

- Here's a bit of juicy gossip. Remember Catherine the Great, our former fair and just leader who would have you beheaded for calling her "Catherine the Conventional"?

- Since her death last month, some folks have been implying she didn't actually die of natural causes. She died—how can I put this gently—while doing the dirty deed with a male member of the equine persuasion.

- Is that a fair accusation? For all we know she and the horse were just friends.

- Yes, Catherine had between twelve and twenty-two male lovers throughout her life, but who among us hasn't been on a date and been told to get in line and take a number?

- Quite honestly, if my name ended with "the Great," you better believe I'd use it to get my Debauchery Card punched.

- The one I feel sorry for is the guy she might have dumped before the horse. How do you compete with that?

- We'll never know what really happened. But I'd hate to see a reputation tarnished by one tiny impulsive act where you end up being accidentally crushed while having relations with a farm animal.

1815 AD
Napoleon Bonaparte Exiled to the Island of St. Helena

- Our Emperor Napoleon loses at the Battle of Waterloo; is forced to abdicate; and now has been exiled to the island of St. Helena. Worse yet, his new title is Imperial Majesty, Emperor of Nothing in Particular.

- It's not easy going from "Emperor of the French" to "Lord of the Water Closet."

- One minute you're commanding thousands of soldiers. The next minute your caretaker is telling you, "Peel your own damn grape!"

- The only mail he now receives is addressed to "Abdicated Occupant."

- Word is Napoleon has begun writing his memoir. It's expected to be over 500 pages long. Twenty pages without the I's, Me's, and My Highnesses.

- We'll know he's no longer obsessing about ruling the world when he changes his Napoleonic Code to allow talking with your mouth full.

- The big question: Will he finally appreciate having some time to relax, or begin organizing an army of sea crabs to invade Russia?

1830 AD
First Steam-Powered Passenger Railway Begins Service

- The Liverpool and Manchester Railway, the world's first entirely steam-powered railroad, began service. It's so revolutionary the engineers still whip the boiler while yelling, "Onward!"

- Before, you had to ride in horse-drawn carriages packed with a few other travelers. Now you can ride squeezed in with twenty-five sweating and pungent people.

- The trains have first- and second-class passenger sections— or as the first class calls the second class, breathing cargo.

- Dignitaries on the first ride included the Prime Minister the Duke of Wellington and the Austrian ambassador—plus an Aberdeen Angus that traces its roots to the House of Udder.

- The railway travels over specially built bridges—each one designed to withstand the weight of cattle and of passengers nicknamed Lord Lard Bottom or Dutchess of Pork Pie.

- The train also runs through a number of neighborhoods. In fact, in three minutes it's due to barrel down our theatre's center aisle.

- We were going to interview the engineer on the first trip, but he was unable to dislodge the sparrow that flew into his mouth.

1848 AD
Karl Marx and Friedrich Engels Publish *Communist Manifesto*

- Two guys named Marx and Engels published a twenty-three-page pamphlet called the *Communist Manifesto*—or as most people call a twenty-three-page pamphlet, twenty-two pages too long.

- The pamphlet isn't exactly a laugh-fest. Picture Marx and Engels as a comedy team with two straight men.

- Why is this dour duo so down on free enterprise—particularly when the job market is desperate for more political philosophers?

- The *Communist Manifesto* talks about class struggle and the evils of capitalism. Really? I've never heard one complaint from my writing team of indentured scribblers.

- Perhaps there are some advantages to a classless society—especially for anyone who's ever been told they have no class.

- Marx and Engels' message, however, seems to be catching on. Last night, my assistant producer yelled at me, "Hey buddy, it's 'Mr. Oppressed Class' to you!"

- Someone must be reading the *Communist Manifesto*. I notice the Applause sign now reads "Rise up and overthrow the tyrant host."

From the Desk

1843 AD

5 Early Draft Endings of Charles Dickens' *A Christmas Carol*

- Ebenezer Scrooge awakens on Christmas, now fluent in twelve languages.

- Ebenezer Scrooge is paid a visit by the Ghost of Christmas Past Participle.

- Ebenezer Scrooge awakens in the arms of a lovable floozy named Carla.

- Ebenezer Scrooge gives Bob Cratchit an increase in pay, minus quill and ink rental fees.

- Ebenezer Scrooge awakens a changed man, but still longs for the old Ebenezer *je ne sais quoi.*

1859 AD
Darwin Publishes
On the Origin of Species

- Have you read this book *On the Origin of Species* by Charles Darwin? Apparently, my description of my brother-in-law as an incompetent baboon isn't that far off.

- The book talks about something called "natural selection," also referred to as survival of the fittest. I'd like to think there are reasons for us being here other than one of our distant relatives outwrestled a clam.

- Ladies, would you go out with any man who asks, "Care to come back to my place and evolve?"

- And men, you might think twice before allowing friends to fix you up with a gal named Petula Platypus.

- Darwin married his cousin, Emma Wedgwood. I'm no biologist but this sounds more like the survival of the creepiest.

- The Church of England has criticized Darwin because his theory contradicts the belief in divine creation. Well, I do find it hard to believe God created my mother-in-law.

- Darwin did a lot of research on the Galápagos Islands. Can we pause here and give the cue card guy a round of applause for correctly spelling Galápagos?

1882 AD
Queen Victoria Survives 8th Assassination Attempt

- Queen Victoria survived her eighth assassination attempt by a crazy man. It's time to bar anyone being near her majesty who's wearing a casual straitjacket.

- The latest nut, Roderick Maclean, was quickly taken into custody. He immediately demanded an interior decorator for his padded cell.

- How crazy is he? You could fill an insane asylum with just the voices in his head.

- Queen Victoria was the first bride to wear a white wedding dress. It probably should've been a white, bulletproof wedding dress.

- The first assassination attempt on the Queen was in 1840, when Edward Oxford fired at her with his dueling pistol. It was the greatest achievement in Oxford's life next to successfully inserting a spoonful of soup in the correct orifice.

- The crazies are everywhere. This theatre now has three seating sections: orchestra, balcony and looney bin.

- Fortunately, at less than five feet tall, Queen Victoria is a small target. In fact, she's the only guest we've had on the show who required a royal booster seat.

1896 AD
Sigmund Freud Founds Psychoanalysis

- Dr. Sigmund Freud, an Austrian neurologist, has developed a method of figuring out what's going wrong inside your head. It could replace the old method of asking, "Are you crazy?"

- He's in such demand as a psychiatrist, he's booking three patients at a time on each couch.

- Freud thinks human behavior is influenced by unconscious memories—something to remind people the next time they say, "I have no memory of borrowing money from you."

- He says unconscious memories, thoughts and urges influence our lives in ways we're not even aware of—which could also explain why we giggle when someone says "Wienerschnitzel."

- Freud believes something called the "psyche" is made up of the id, the ego, and the superego. And I thought id, ego and superego was just a weird law firm.

- He says when wishes can't be fulfilled in our waking lives, they are carried out in dreams. For example, last night I had a dream you'd be laughing at this joke.

- Freud also believes in something called the Oedipus complex, which is when a child feels, how should I say this, attracted to the parent of the opposite sex. Good night, everybody.

1911 AD
Marie Curie Awarded Second Nobel Prize

- Marie Curie has been awarded the Nobel Prize in Chemistry, proving once again a woman's place is in the home—if the home is full of test tubes and Bunsen burners.

- Curie also became the first person to receive two Nobel Prizes—three if you count winning the Royal Swedish Academy of Sciences' Guess Your Weight contest.

- She won for her studies in polonium and radium. And like any good parent, she never favors one element over the other.

- Marie and husband Pierre won the 1903 Physics Nobel for their joint research on radiation phenomena. Most married couples can't even agree on how to spell "phenomena."

- She discovered the element "polonium," which she named after her native country, Poland. That's classy. I would've named it after a winning horse that paid two-to-one odds.

- The Curies also invented the word "radioactive"—a shortened term for "Don't touch anything that glows in the dark."

- Marie and Pierre Curie published thirty-two scientific papers between 1898 and 1902—not including their best seller, *101 Delicious Dishes Made from Polonium.*

5 Worst Things About Being Jack the Ripper

- You're a generous spender, but no one calls you Jack the Tipper.

- Your mail keeps getting delivered to the other Jack the Ripper.

- No restaurant will hold a table for "The Ripper party."

- That "What have you been up to?" question at school reunions.

- People never get to really know the real Jack the Ripper.

Chapter 3:
Here's One for the American History Books.

1521 AD
Juan Ponce de León Searches for the Fountain of Youth

- There's a story going around that explorer Ponce de León, who recently died, discovered the Fountain of Youth in the new world. And who better to verify a story about living forever than a guy who didn't live long enough to tell you about it?

- Apparently, he was about to announce it, but became confused when he reached puberty again.

- They say the fountain's water has healing powers that mysteriously maintain your youthful appearance, because what elderly person doesn't want to have a baby face?

- While searching for the Fountain of Youth, Ponce de León discovered a place nearby called Florida, which had a hotel that rented by the day, week or eternity.

- Living forever has its downsides. What will you say when your wife asks, "Will you love me when I'm 650?"

- If you want to know what living forever feels like, try standing up here after a joke bombs.

- In honor of Ponce de León, we'll be giving out free tickets to our show, good for any night in 500 years.

1616 AD
Pocahontas and John Smith

- Everyone is talking about those crazy kids Pocahontas and Captain John Smith—or as they call them in Jamestown, "ye it couple."

- It's never easy making a relationship work when your family refers to your girlfriend as an "adorable noble savage."

- Smith was first attracted to Pocahontas when she stopped her father, Chief Wahunsenacawh of the Powhatan tribe, from executing him. Also, she had a cute smile.

- Pocahontas was eleven years old when they met, but keep in mind she had the poise and grace of a thirteen-year-old.

- But she grew tired of waiting for John to pop the question and married a warrior named Kocoum. Who could blame her? Would you want to be an old maid at fifteen?

- Pocahontas next married a tobacco planter named John Rolfe and converted to Christianity. Many think she did it to make John Smith jealous—and for the "Mrs. Noble Savage" monogrammed towels.

- We haven't given up on getting Pocahontas and John Smith back together. In fact, we'd like to have them on the show sometime—after the typhoid epidemic and before the next famine.

1621 AD
Native American Reaction to First Thanksgiving

- Have you run into any of these people calling themselves Pilgrims who recently arrived in a boat called the *Mayflower*? Talk about a clueless crew. No "Hello," no "How are you?" Just "How do we grow corn?"

- And why the big funny hats with the weird buckle when an understated feather will perfectly complete the outfit?

- They've renamed our land "Plymouth Colony." Given their pale complexions and general ill health, they should've called it Scurvyville.

- Are you getting tired of their endless questions about planting, growing and hunting? It's like they say, give a man a fish and you feed him for a day; teach a man to fish and he'll get sick of eating fish.

- The Pilgrims seem nice enough, but can you really trust anyone who describes himself as a "puritan"? I mean, who among us hasn't lusted for another man's squaw?

- Squanto, you know what I'm talking about.

- Any of you going to their Thanksgiving dinner? I will be out of there so fast if they seat me at the Wampanoag children's table.

First Tavern Established in America

- Samuel Cole has opened the first tavern in the American Colonies. Finally, a place people can go for a drink and forget about smallpox, diphtheria and hookworms.

- Cole arrived in New England with John Winthrop in 1630. Winthrop was a co-founder of the Massachusetts Bay Colony. Cole founded two-ales-for-the-price-of-one night.

- Before Cole's Tavern opened in Boston, folks would sit in the woods, drink a pint and pour out their troubles to an empathetic raccoon.

- He's created lots of new jobs for the community—including designated teetotalers.

- Recently, Governor Henry Vane brought the Narragansett Indian sachem Miantonomoh, with his retinue, for a meal at Cole's Tavern. Someone said, "How can you bring that savage in here?" and Miantonomoh said, "Back off, he's my friend."

- We're thinking about serving drinks on our show—as long as I don't have to listen to some guest drone on about an evil spirit forcing his wife to pledge her soul to the devil.

- Our show will be coming from Cole's Tavern next week. My guests will be ye olde Grammarian and ye olde Linguist who will debate that age-old argument, Thee versus Thou.

5 Firsts for Harvard's First Graduating Class

- First and last class with no legacy students

- First person named Saltonstall accepted without the assistance of another person named Saltonstall

- First student placed on probation for attending spring ball with a witch

- First student to call the *Mayflower* his family yacht

- First party-hearty student nicknamed the Pukin' Puritan

1752 AD
Benjamin Franklin Discovers Connection Between Lightning and Electricity

- Using a kite during a thunderstorm, Ben Franklin demonstrated the connection between lightning and electricity—and he's got the charred fingers to prove it.

- Testing his theory with his son, he also demonstrated he could use a few lessons in responsible parenting.

- The kite was attached to a metal house key. As it rose in the air, all you could hear was the wind and his wife yelling, "Hey, I'm locked out of the house!"

- The kite wasn't struck by lightning, but did pick up electrical charges in the atmosphere, so Ben only vibrated like a hummingbird.

- Ben is now working on something called a lightning rod. How about a more useful invention like an extra-large fork for eating cherry pie?

- Ben Franklin will be here tomorrow to explain some more of his scientific theories and, hopefully, show us his still-smoldering wig.

1775 AD
Paul Revere's Midnight Ride

- The American Revolution kicked off this week with much credit to our roving patriot Paul Revere—and he's got the saddle sores to prove it.

- By eavesdropping around town and in pubs, he learned about the British plans to march on Concord. His best source was a barmaid known as Lascivious Lucy, the loose Loyalist.

- Revere was also notified of the British movements by a lantern signal from Boston's North Church: one if by land, two if by sea, three if undecided but leaning towards one.

- Two lanterns indicated the British heading to Concord on the Charles River. Revere also overheard a lazy British oarsman complain, "Would it kill them to take the land route?"

- In no time, Revere was galloping through the countryside shouting, "The Regulars are coming out. The Regulars are coming out"—and then "I'm hoarse, I need a drink of water. I'm hoarse, I need a drink of water."

- Realizing they were outnumbered, the Redcoats retreated back to Boston, screaming, "The Regulars are coming back! The Regulars are coming back!"

- We asked Paul to be a guest tonight. He replied, "I have a previous engagement! I have a previous engagement!"

1776 AD
Thomas Paine's *Common Sense*

- The pamphlet *Common Sense* has everyone thinking about the colonies declaring independence. We've tried working things out with England. Maybe it's time we started seeing other countries.

- The forty-seven-page pamphlet was written by a secret writer who calls himself "Republicus." I believe Republicus was also the Greek god of Long Wind.

- In addition to being sold to countless readers, *Common Sense* has been read aloud at taverns and meeting places—also by town criers who've run out of things to cry.

- In *Common Sense*, the author calls for independence from England and the creation of a democratic republic. He also includes a terrific recipe for Yorkshire pudding.

- *Common Sense* makes such a persuasive case for independence, last night my wife declared sovereignty from her side of the bed.

- I was going to read the entire forty-seven-page *Common Sense* on our show, but during rehearsal our cue card guy collapsed with a hernia.

- We are thinking about having Republicus on the show. We're still waiting to hear from his manager, Fifteen Percenticus.

1776 AD
U.S. Declares Independence

- Our Thirteen Colonies have declared independence from England. Bad news for anyone who just bought one of those "World's Greatest Monarch" tea cups.

- Even worse news if you're expecting your employees to work on the Fourth of July.

- The Declaration was drawn up by the Second Continental Congress meeting in Philadelphia. It would've taken less time, but they spent days looking for a word that rhymed with "unalienable."

- Thomas Jefferson, Mr. Smarty Breeches, composed the original draft. We all went to school with guys like him—the ones who'd never let you copy off their calligraphy.

- We're now called the United States of America—although two founders from Massachusetts, who will remain anonymous, lobbied pretty hard for "Adamsville."

- The document lists our grievances against King George III— not including objections to his wardrobe and white wig.

- The Declaration of Independence includes, "We hold these truths to be self-evident, that all men are created equal." Tell that to our audience members sitting up in the nosebleed seats.

5 Signs You Are a Salem Witch Possessed by The Devil

- You've signed up for a caldron-stirring workshop.

- You've named your children Lucyfer, and Beelzebubala.

- Your Puritan ideals of self-control and discipline have been supplanted by slow waltzing with bobcats and squirrels.

- You've started speaking in tongues, and your tongues speak perfect Latin.

- You are haunted each night by an evil spirit that repeatedly wails, "Stop hogging the blanket."

1780 AD
Benedict Arnold Deserts Colonial Army

- Before I begin tonight's monologue, does anybody want to buy some really old heroic Benedict Arnold jokes?

- Remember Benedict Arnold, Revolutionary War hero? Now he's Benedict Arnold, traitor. Even his horse threw him in disgust.

- After recently being appointed commander of the American fort at West Point, he plotted to surrender it to the British in return for money and a new title, General Benedict Judas.

- Some say Arnold's new, young wife, Peggy Shippen, a Tory, influenced his decision to desert. In fact, she constantly complained to him, "We never defect anywhere together."

- Arnold claims while serving in the Continental Army he never received the recognition and encouragement he deserved. It's true. Not once did anyone pat him on the back and say, "Who's a good traitor? You're a good traitor."

- Many of his fellow officers found Benedict Arnold to be vain, emotional and greedy—or as my staff calls that, me.

- We've had sword-swallowers, acrobats, and tumblers on our show. But we've never had someone like Benedict Arnold, a master at juggling loyalties.

1782 AD
Bald Eagle Adopted by Congress as the National Bird

- Congress has declared the American bald eagle our national bird—no doubt because it has friends in high places.

- The 1776 Continental Congress told Ben Franklin, Tom Jefferson and John Adams to design our nation's first official seal, but they couldn't agree on anything that would win approval—not even one that said "World's Best Congress."

- Congress then asked Philadelphia artist William Barton to give it a try. He came up with a design that included a white eagle after failing to get a hummingbird to sit still for a portrait.

- They eventually went with the bald eagle because it's indigenous only to North America, whereas the white eagle gets around—if you know what I mean.

- Benjamin Franklin says the eagle is "a bird of bad moral character." I don't even want to know how he found that out.

- Many see the bald eagle as a symbol of strength, courage, freedom and immortality. That's putting a lot of pressure on one bird.

- As for me, I'm for any national bird as long as it's served with string beans and potatoes.

1788 AD
U.S. Constitution Ratified

- Our nation now has a constitution—which beats the old way of governing: deciding legislation with card games and cockfights.

- It establishes America's national government and fundamental laws, and guarantees certain basic rights for its citizens—although our audience is still prohibited from using the person sitting in front of you as a spittoon.

- The Constitution takes the place of the Articles of Confederation, which took the place of some rules scribbled on the back of a tobacco wrapper.

- The document was signed by delegates at the Constitutional Convention in Philadelphia. In addition, half of them also added a gratuity.

- John Hancock, whose signature was prominently displayed in the Declaration of Independence, wasn't at the Convention. That meant more signing room for everyone else.

- The Constitution contains seven articles—eight if you count updated rules for whist.

- Under the new Constitution, the federal government will have three branches, ensuring if anything goes wrong, each branch will be able to blame the other two.

George Washington Inaugurated as First U.S. President

- Today, our country inaugurated its first president, George Washington. After years of complaining about British rule, we at last can complain about American rule.

- President Washington has always been known for being truthful. Now that he's an elected politician, let's see how long he can go without telling a lie.

- The moment when it really felt like we were no longer a British colony was when someone yelled "The Redcoats aren't coming! The Redcoats aren't coming!"

- Washington's wife, Martha, is now the First Lady—actually the first, First Lady.

- The ceremony began on the balcony of Federal Hall in New York City. It was kind of like Romeo and Juliet if Juliet looked like Vice President John Adams.

- Adams was inaugurated as vice president nine days ago. Apparently, he wanted first dibs on the bigger office.

- He hasn't served one day, but we can say with absolute certainty George Washington is the best president we've ever had.

From the Desk

1775 AD

5 Rejected Battle of Bunker Hill Orders to Troops

- Don't fire until you see the wine stains on their lapels.

- Don't fire until you've worked up a sufficient amount of anger and resentment.

- Don't fire until you've really given this a lot of thought.

- Don't fire if your hearts are not really in it.

- Don't fire until I can get everyone together for a group portrait.

1791 AD
Whiskey Rebellion

- Farmers in Western Pennsylvania are leading a "Whiskey Rebellion." Their battle cry is, "Don't fire until you see the whites of their bloodshot eyes."

- The Whiskey Rebellion is like the Boston Tea Party but with more of a kick to it.

- The farmers are protesting Congress's approval of a new federal tax on spirits and the stills that produce them. They've raised their glasses and said, "We'll riot to that."

- It's the first tax imposed on a domestic product by our newly formed federal government. But only whiskey? Apparently, we have a pretty powerful lemonade lobby.

- Many resisters are Revolutionary War veterans, which may explain why many are calling this rebellion "The Whiskey Shot Heard 'Round the World."

- The farmers believe the tax unfairly targets one region over others. That wouldn't be the case if you could go into a tavern and order a hearty mug of Vermont maple syrup.

- Let's hope Congress doesn't look at this uprising and say, "Hey, let's charge a rebellion tax."

1803 AD
Louisiana Purchase

- The recent Louisiana Purchase from France added 828,000 square miles to our country—giving every man, woman and child in the U.S. more room to get away from their relatives.

- French Emperor Napoleon Bonaparte decided to sell us the territory after buying it only five years ago. Apparently, he had conqueror's remorse.

- The total purchase cost was fifteen million dollars. I'm not saying President Jefferson overpaid, but I know a guy who could've gotten him Portugal for fifty bucks and a freshly plucked chicken.

- The U.S. had to borrow money to buy the territory. In fact, we're using New Jersey as collateral.

- The purchase extends the U.S. across the Mississippi River, nearly doubling our country's size. That explains why settlers in one of these distant territories have declared themselves the state of "Middle of Nowhere."

- The objective driving this deal was acquiring the Mississippi River port of New Orleans—which will make us a world shipping leader and number one breeder of mosquitos.

- I've also asked our landlord to expand our theatre, with very affordable back-row seats in Missouri.

Lewis and Clark Expedition

- Lewis and Clark returned from their 8,000-mile expedition, exploring lands west of the Mississippi River. They brought back eighty-three newly created maps and a ton of dirty laundry.

- President Jefferson appointed Meriwether Lewis the Expedition Commander and William Clark Executive Vice Chief in Charge of Logistics and Flannel Shirts.

- Their journey took two years. This is why they didn't send a husband-and-wife team—it would've definitely been a relationship breaker.

- The expedition encountered about fifty Native American tribes. That means they had to learn fifty different ways to say, "Help! We don't know where the hell we are!"

- Although Lewis and Clark failed to find a Northwest Passage water route across the continent, they did find a little Sioux bed & breakfast to die for—and didn't.

- During their trip, they identified at least 120 animal specimens—which wasn't easy since many were also man-eating specimens.

- In honor of Lewis and Clark's magnificent achievement, we're giving everyone in our audience a free compass and map to help find their way back to the lobby.

1823 AD
Monroe Doctrine

- During his State of the Union Address, President Monroe announced his new doctrine which opposes European colonialism in the Western Hemisphere. However, not before a conquistador declared his podium part of Spain.

- Secretary of State John Quincy Adams is the actual author of Monroe's doctrine. Although, Monroe came up with the basic idea when he asked Adams, "Is your doctor in?"

- The doctrine says any intervention in the Americas by foreign powers is a potentially hostile act against the United States—particularly if you don't say, "May I please intervene?"

- In return, the U.S. pledges to recognize and not interfere with the internal affairs of European countries. After all, do we really care whose fault it is Italy is shaped like a big boot?

- As far back as 1783, the U.S. adopted the policy of isolation. Our nation's first motto was, "We'd really like to be alone."

- It's time we told the world to stop colonizing the Americas. Last night, I asked for my usual restaurant table. They said they couldn't because it was just claimed by France.

- Our show has its own doctrine. It substitutes "opposing intervention in the political affairs of the Americas" with "opposing anyone who refuses to laugh at our lame jokes."

From the Desk
1779 AD

5 Rejected John Paul Jones Replies to Surrender

- I have not yet had even ten minutes to think this over.

- I have not yet conferred with my Ouija board.

- I have not yet allowed time for my hardtack to digest.

- I have not yet coordinated my silk breeches with my ruffle cuffs.

- You again?

Chapter 4:
But Seriously, Is This a Great Country or What?

1825 AD
Erie Canal Completed

- The 364-mile Erie Canal across New York state has been completed. It would've been shorter, but they had to dig around wolves, bears and one angry moose.

- You can now ride a boat from New York City, up the Hudson River to Albany and across the state to Lake Erie. Of course, you may have to share a stateroom with a sack of barley.

- The canal's most ardent advocate is governor and former New York City mayor DeWitt Clinton. He got the idea after tiring of transporting state senators in his back pocket.

- Canal construction began in 1817 and was supervised by men with no formal training as engineers. In fact, their only experience was meticulously observing a colony of beavers.

- To celebrate the opening, Clinton dumped two kegs of Lake Erie water into Long Island Sound—after which a lobster popped out of the water and said, "Tastes like Lake Ontario."

- The canal has lowered the cost of moving freight, thus making it the favored mode of transportation for grain, lumber and plumpish passengers.

- We're so inspired by this amazing engineering achievement we're now digging a canal from our lobby to the popcorn stand.

1846 AD
Anesthesia Used in Major Operation

- The first major operation using anesthesia was performed. The medical community is calling it a non-screaming success.

- They removed a tumor from the neck of a patient who didn't feel a thing. However, he did yelp when the doctor attempted to extract payment from his wallet.

- The operation was performed at Massachusetts General Hospital in Boston. Its motto until now has been "Stop shrieking. The neighbors are complaining."

- Patients used to need opium, alcohol or a bullet to bite on to deal with excruciating pain. Now all they need is something to warm up the ice-cold bed pans.

- Using sulfuric ether, the patient didn't feel a thing. Wow! A drug that totally knocks you out. My bartender has been administering it for years.

- An earlier attempt to use the anesthesia ended in failure when the patient cried out in agony. More specifically, he cried out, "I just have an ingrown toenail!"

- Surgery has certainly advanced. In the old days they used saws, knives and sharp hooks—and that was just for notifying people visiting hours were over.

1847 AD
Donner Party

- We've finally heard from the Donner Party, those pioneers who migrated to California in a wagon train from the Midwest. And believe me when I tell you, their story is hard to swallow.

- Right from the beginning the trip left a bad taste in a lot of people's mouths.

- After spending the winter of 1846 and 1847 snowbound in the Sierra Nevada mountain range and running out of food, they, uh, well, let's just say they went from "love thy neighbor" to "love thy neighbor with a sprinkling of salt."

- I've heard of people borrowing a cup of sugar from their friend Ethel, but not a cup *of* Ethel.

- Trouble began when the party decided to take a new route called the Hastings Cutoff—which is ironic, since trouble got worse when a guy named Hasting woke up and found part of himself cut off.

- By the end of their journey, ten people had the same nickname, Stumpy.

- I just want to emphasize to our audience, our refreshments of beans and franks do not contain anyone named Frank.

1848 AD
John B. Curtis Invents
Chewing Gum

- A man named John B. Curtis has invented something called chewing gum—as if we need another bad habit in addition to spitting and only bathing during leap year.

- It's the first commercially sold chewing product. Previously, people had to gnaw on anything they could find and hope it didn't bite back.

- Curtis's product is called State of Maine Pure Spruce Gum— for people who love the wonderful aftertaste of tree bark.

- The gum is made from sticky spruce tree resin, and if you thought being locked in a kiss was romantic, wait until you've been locked in a kiss for two weeks.

- The gum is sold on little sticks, wrapped in tissue paper— with clearly written instructions: "Chew the gum, not the stick or tissue paper."

- It's hard to look sophisticated and debonair while chewing gum—unless your butler is chomping on it for you.

- We gave some gum to our staff. Within minutes, they sounded like a herd of cud-chewing cows.

1811 AD

5 Things Daniel Boone Does Not Want You to Know

- Calling him "Danny" makes him blush.

- He will not relieve himself in the woods if he thinks a raccoon is watching.

- During his three terms in the Virginia General Assembly, he was frequently censored for wearing buckskin breeches.

- He originally wanted to name Boonesborough, the town he founded, Booneyville.

- Although he's a great trailblazing explorer, in the bedroom his wife has to shout directions.

1848 AD
California Gold Rush

- They've discovered gold at a place called Sutter's Mill in Coloma, California. Overnight, penniless bums have become penniless bums panning for gold.

- They're calling this "Gold Gever"—which shouldn't be confused with silver scoliosis.

- Everyone is heading west to strike it rich. The line of people streaming into California is so long, the last guy is still waiting in Utah.

- James Marshall, who made the discovery, was building a sawmill for Sutter when he found shiny flakes of gold in the river—and two bears jumping up and down, growling, "We're rich!"

- At first, Marshall and Sutter were able to keep news of the discovery under wraps—until they changed their names to Fat Cat and Money Bags.

- The entire area is now covered with gold miners. In fact, one prospector woke from his nap to find another pounding a claim stake into his bellybutton.

- Some of our staff quit to seek their fortune in California. One unsuccessful panner was last spotted on a street corner with a sign reading, "Will write one-liners for food."

1850 AD
Emily Dickinson

- We originally planned to have poet Emily Dickinson on the show. However, we had no idea she was a total recluse. Her idea of a night out on the town is a leisurely walk to the end of her hallway.

- We were also told she only speaks to visitors through doors, and I'm not about to start an interview with "knock knock."

- Many of Miss Dickinson's poems are about death and immortality—which is why she's still on the fence about buying life insurance.

- Emily does, however, maintain many relationships through writing letters. In fact, she's been courted by at least five men who work at the post office.

- Because she doesn't get out much, people around town referred to her as "the Myth"—which explains her favorite phrase, "I myth you so much."

- Some people think she prefers solitude so she can focus on her inner world and her creativity. Others think she just likes listening to crickets.

- Too bad we couldn't get her on the show. I was hoping to talk to her about poetry—and why isn't there a word that rhymes with orange.

1853 AD
Elisha Otis Invents the Elevator

- Tonight's guest is Elisha Otis who's invented a contraption called the elevator. It's a tiny room that moves people up and down in buildings. Do you know what this means? We can now experience what it's like to be a plate of baked potatoes riding in a dumbwaiter.

- Can you imagine feeling a room rising and lowering without having one drink?

- The elevator is pulled up and down with a thin metal cable strong enough to support at least three pianos or four overweight relatives.

- Envision the interesting conversations you'll have riding down from the fourth floor: "How are you?" "Nice hat." "Do you think we'll crash?"

- Here's a thought: How about putting a small band in the elevator for background music—or at the very least, a guy who can nose whistle "Farewell My Lilly Dear."

- I'd install one, if only to lower me into the pit where my writers work.

- According to Mr. Otis, orders for his elevator have been flying in—as well as messages saying, "Help, were stuck between the third and fourth floors!"

1854 AD
Henry David Thoreau

- Henry David Thoreau was supposed to be our guest tonight. However, he canceled because we refused to give "Mr. Self-Reliance" a ride to the theatre.

- Thoreau lives in a little shack he built outside Concord, Massachusetts, at Walden Pond so he can be closer to nature—especially one chipmunk he claims gives him investment advice.

- He's an advocate of transcendentalism, the belief in the inherent goodness of people and nature—except for one neighbor who borrowed his lucky ax and hasn't returned it.

- Thoreau also believes in civil disobedience—as long as your spouse doesn't catch you civilly disobeying your wedding vows.

- While fending for himself in his little hut, his mother helps him with food and doing his laundry. I don't recall Davy Crockett's mom combing out the tail of his coonskin cap.

- Every morning, Thoreau takes a bath in the pond and calls it a religious experience—particularly when he can find a helpful otter to scrub his back.

- We really wish Thoreau had come tonight—especially since we replaced the guest chair with a giant toadstool.

1869 AD
Completion of First Transcontinental Railroad

- They finally finished the Transcontinental Railroad. At last, you can ride coast to coast while sitting next to a guy with a chicken on his lap.

- The ceremony culminated as the presidents of the Union Pacific and Central Pacific railroads pounded a gold spike into the rail line. Five minutes later, a prospector parked his mule on it and staked a claim.

- The two railroads would've been joined sooner, but one line accidentally ended up in Canada.

- They didn't realize they'd made a mistake until they inadvertently linked up with a team of sled dogs.

- Before this new railroad connection, it could take up to six months to cross the country—seven if your horse breast-stroked across the Mississippi River.

- The railroad companies also worked out a deal with the U.S. Postal Service. All retired Pony Express horses can now ride for free.

- Call me old-fashioned, but no transcontinental trip is complete without circling the wagons at night and having a trail guide named Gabby bore you with campfire stories.

5 Samuel Morse Draft Telegraph Messages

- Is this thing on?

- What are you wearing?

- I am the telegraph king.

- I am a man of few dots and dashes.

- Put your mother on the line.

1876 AD
James-Younger Gang Robs Bank

- Jesse James and his James-Younger Gang rode into Northfield, Minnesota to rob the First National Bank—and illegally hitching their horses in a loading zone was the least of their problems

- After a gun battle, the few gang members who managed to escape left with only $26.70. James hasn't stolen that little since he cracked open his brother's piggy bank.

- This is shocking, since Jesse James robs banks like most people eat beans.

- He's the only outlaw who calls holdup notes withdrawal slips.

- The First National Bank is said to be the largest west of the Mississippi River. In fact, three of the robbers got lost walking across the lobby.

- Jesse's father was a preacher, although he was the only clergyman who preached "Thou shall not steal anything smaller than a ten-dollar bill."

- People have compared Jesse James to Robin Hood. Really? I can't imagine Merry Men carrying six-shooters.

- We actually considered inviting Jesse on our show to talk about the botched robbery. However, we don't have a safe place to keep our petty cash.

1879 AD
Thomas Edison Invents the Light Bulb

- How depressing is it that a candle can no longer hold a candle to a light bulb?

- Inventor Thomas Edison has developed a long-lasting electric light bulb that can be used for practical purposes. The bad news? Jack B. Nimble now has to find a word that rhymes with "filament lamp."

- This was also a bad week for magician The Great Paraffinoni, Wizard of Wax.

- How do you even turn off a light bulb? I mean, there's no place to blow on it.

- Can you imagine campers listening to ghost stories while sitting around a flickering bulb?

- It might be a great invention, if only the electric light bulb didn't come with a monthly electric light bill.

- Edison has also formed the Edison Electric Light Company to promote his next invention, his ability to print money.

- I suppose I'll eventually switch to light bulbs, but only when I can use them to light my cigars.

1879 AD
Invention of the Telephone

- I'm sure you've all heard about this new thing called the telephone invented by Alexander Graham Bell. It actually allows you to talk with another person at another location, without screaming, "Hey, dummy, over here!"

- This is also a great device for you folks whose teenagers are always tapping away on the telegraph.

- Plus, it eliminates being put on hold when sending smoke signals.

- Already, my staff is working on phone conversations like, "I swear honey, the phone makes me sound much shorter."

- The first words Bell spoke into the phone were, "Mr. Watson, come here—I want to see you." Really? I think I would've gone the prank route with, "Hey Watson, help me. I'm stuck in this little box!"

- And Bell has even bigger plans. By next year he wants to start charging people for long-distance calls beyond seventy-five feet.

- But you know what the greatest thing about the telephone is? You can talk to anyone while wearing only your long johns.

5 Rejected Titles for the Book
Moby Dick

- Michael Dick

- Moby, Moby Not

- The Annoying Captain Ahab

- Spouting Off

- The Agony and the Blubbery

1881 AD
Billy the Kid Gunned Down

- Outlaw Billy the Kid was shot by Sheriff Pat Garrett at the Maxwell Ranch in New Mexico—or as most people call it when a desperado is killed, death by natural causes.

- Billy the Kid's real name was Henry McCarty. However, the nickname Henry the Kid was already taken by a notorious carrot-stealing goat.

- Billy the Kid was the most wanted man in the West; although, he was the least wanted for courting your daughter.

- In court, Judge Warren Bristol said to Billy, "I sentence you to hang, until you are dead, dead, dead." They don't call him the stuttering judge for nothing.

- Billy responded, "And you can go to hell, hell, hell." The judge then tacked on an additional charge for stealing his shtick.

- Billy had escaped from prison only days before his scheduled execution. He tricked his jailors into letting him go coffin shopping.

- Garrett found Billy's hideout and hid in his bedroom. When Billy entered, Garrett shot him dead—or as they're now calling it, the worst surprise party ever.

1881 AD
Gunfight at the O.K. Corral

- There was a gunfight yesterday at the O.K. Corral. It makes you wonder, why can't horses get along?

- The shootout involved the Earp brothers and Doc Holliday against the Cochise County Cowboys—Billy Claiborne and the Clanton and McLaury brothers. Introductions alone took two hours.

- There are three Earp brothers: Virgil, Morgan and Wyatt. Normally, when you hear three Earps, it's after someone has eaten some bad chili.

- The Clantons and McLaurys are cattle rustlers, thieves and murderers—or as their proud parents call them, multifaceted.

- The gunfight was the result of a long-simmering feud. In fact, they even argued over calling it a disagreement or a dispute.

- The Earp brothers and Doc Holliday claimed the Cowboys opened fire after they tried to disarm them for illegally carrying firearms. Given the results, I would've gone with a strongly worded note.

- Frankly, I'm getting tired of all this violence and mayhem. I mean, why not the pie eating contest at the O.K. Corral?

1886 AD
Coca-Cola Invented

- Have you tried the new drink, Coca-Cola? It tastes so good, after a hundred sips, you'll still want more.

- Its inventor, John Stith Pemberton, claims it'll cure everything including indigestion, nerve disorders, headaches and impotence—with a bitter aftertaste that only lasts twenty years.

- Pemberton was a Confederate officer who was wounded in the Civil War and became addicted to morphine—which explains his first, failed product, "Uncle Pemberton's Morphine-flavored Pies."

- Coca-Cola is being marketed as a patent medicine. In fact, most doctors are telling their patients "Drink 300 bottles and telegraph me in the morning."

- Since Coca-Cola is carbonated, it gives you that wonderful feeling of a pack of wasps fighting their way out of your mouth.

- It's made from the coca leaf and the kola nut and has no harmful side effects. In fact, my writers have stayed up for weeks drinking it with no noticeable side effects.

- Coca-Cola is called the temperance drink because it contains no alcohol. Can I get 1,000 jumpy amens to that?

1886 AD
Statue of Liberty is Unveiled

- The Statue of Liberty, a massive sculpture of a lady holding a torch and a tablet inscribed with the date of our Declaration of Independence, was dedicated today in New York Harbor. The statue's message of freedom is so powerful twelve other statues have already demanded their emancipation.

- The 151-foot-tall figure is a gift from France. It was built there, shipped overseas and assembled here. It would have taken less time to put together had our engineer reading their instructions been fluent in more than French fries.

- The Statue of Liberty was designed by sculptor Frédéric Auguste Bartholdi. He said the hardest part was finding her a pair of size 750 extra-wide shoes.

- Only dignitaries were permitted on the island during the ceremonies. Even seagulls had to know somebody.

- President Grover Cleveland presided over the dedication and was quite the gentleman. He delivered his entire speech without once looking up Lady Liberty's big skirt.

- The event also marked New York's first ticker-tape parade. One thing is for sure, cascading bits of paper are a happy alternative to leaping stockbrokers after a financial crash.

- I asked my staff to come up with a statue that best represents me. The only design they have is me shirtless after a card game.

Buffalo Bill's Wild West Show
at Madison Square Garden

- Buffalo Bill Cody and his Wild West Show are performing at Madison Square Garden. If you're not familiar with buffalos, they're slightly smaller than our typical sewer rats.

- Buffalo Bill's show features cowboys and cowgirls, more than 100 Indians, trick riders, ropers, shooters and many different wild animals—plus the only refreshment stand where you have to kill and skin your own snacks.

- The show includes an attack on a stagecoach. This being New York, the driver pays off the bandits and goes on his way.

- Chief Sitting Bull is also in the show. He almost missed opening night when he lost track of time while getting a massage on Coney Island.

- Also featured is Annie Oakley, who shoots a cigar from her husband's lips. The cue for her to shoot is when he asks, "Where's my dinner?"

- As a young man, Buffalo Bill rode for the Pony Express. In his show, he dazzles the crowd by delivering a package with postage due.

- Many ask, is Cody's show an authentic depiction of the Wild West? It is if the West has overpriced tickets and stale popcorn.

5 Things Pony Express Riders Ask Themselves

- Should this horse have a mail slot?

- What if I rode sidesaddle?

- Am I taking work away from carrier pigeons?

- Is it wrong to use Dear John letters as toilet paper?

- Would that coyote like to hear about my day?

1888 AD
World's First Deodorant

- A company has patented the first deodorant that kills odor-causing bacteria—something people have been looking for since one caveman told another caveman, "Whoa, could you please move to another cave?"

- Use it once and people will no longer assume you clean stables for a living.

- The product is called Mum, as in "Please, Mum, do I have to sit next to that odorous man?"

- Mum is sold as a cream in a jar and applied with your fingertips. It's the perfect gift for any foul, fetid friend.

- If you're not sure you need deodorant, ask yourself, why is your lady acquaintance always waving her fan—even when it's ten below zero?

- Mum comes in three strengths: Regular, Strong and Extra Stench-Stopping.

- Using Mum will definitely make it easier for you to meet members of the opposite sex—or at least a member who isn't wearing a clothespin on their nose.

1892 AD
Lizzie Borden is Acquitted

- The trial of the century ended in Fall River, Massachusetts, with Lizzie Borden being acquitted of killing her father and stepmother with an ax. Her family and friends celebrated—at an extremely safe distance from Lizzie.

- With all the incriminating evidence, people are asking the same question: Is it possible to convict a jury of insanity?

- Even her defense lawyer yelled, "You've got to be kidding!"

- Some people say Lizzie's house is now haunted. In fact, at night an eerie voice can be heard moaning, "I'm a ghost, but I'm no ax murderer."

- Lizzie has never married, but now the trial is behind her perhaps she can find a nice gentleman who will make an honest murderess out of her.

- I think the lesson for all of us is be nice to your parents, shower them with gifts, but for heaven's sake, nothing with sharp edges.

- We're actually thinking of asking Lizzie on as a guest—if we can move my chair two blocks away.

1903 AD
Wright Brothers Fly First Motor-Operated Airplane

- Brothers Orville and Wilbur Wright made the first successful self-propelled sustained flight of a powered, heavier-than-air aircraft—in other words, a flying machine bigger than a giant mockingbird.

- Actually, Orville was the pilot and Wilbur stayed on the ground yelling, "When is it my turn?"

- Their flying machine is called the Wright Flyer, which is certainly a more optimistic name than an earlier version called the Wright Crasher.

- Their aircraft took off in Kitty Hawk, North Carolina, for a flight lasting twelve seconds and flew about ten feet above the ground for 120 feet—just long enough for Orville to realize he'd forgotten to pay his life insurance bill.

- The last time anyone flew that long and high was when our assistant director leaped out of his girlfriend's window after her husband came home early.

- Still not impressed? Try asking a yellow-bellied sapsucker to fly you anywhere.

- The big question is, what are they going to do with this machine? I mean, would you pay to fly from New York to Chicago 120 feet at a time?

From the Desk

1863 AD

5 Worst Stephen Foster Fan Letters

- "When you write a song, what comes first, the lyrics, the music or the dripping sentimentality?"

- "You might feel different if you had my old Kentucky home mortgage."

- "Big deal. I came all the way from Buenos Aires with a guitar on my knee."

- "My wife Jeanie has dark brown hair, and I think it's VERY dream-worthy, thank you."

- "I just returned from way down upon the Swanee River— after an alligator bit my leg off."

1913 AD
President Taft Rescued From Bathtub

- Rumor has it President William Howard Taft, who weighs in at 350 pounds, got stuck in a White House bathtub and needed six men to pull him free. That's a big president.

How big?

- He's so big he buys his suits at a circus tent store.

- He's so big his shadow blocks out Maryland.

- He's so big his motto is "Remember the Main Course."

- He's so big he vetoes any bill that doesn't include a dessert menu.

- He's so big Teddy Roosevelt mistook one of his chins for San Juan Hill.

- He's so big his most important cabinet position is reaching into one for a drumstick.

- He's so big he's not only a trust buster, he's a button popper.

But we love the president.

Acknowledgments

Designer David Lennon created a beautiful book—from cover to cover.

Editor Monique Conrod expertly and gently polished the prose and checked the facts.

Late-night veteran writers Gabe Abelson, Bill Scheft and Joe Toplyn generously offered advice and encouragement.

Friend and artist extraordinaire Sandi St. George was enthusiastic and supportive about this idea from the very beginning.

Jack Curry, known to edit everybody, went beyond punchlines to the heart of the matter.

Wife and writer Monica Collins is my biggest supporter, most honest reviewer and all-around wonderful person.

Also, a big thanks to Harpswell, Maine, where the idea for this book flashed in my noggin while walking along Casco Bay on a beautiful sunny morning.

And, of course, Dexter.

www.ingramcontent.com/pod-product-compliance
Lightning Source LLC
Chambersburg PA
CBHW070728130626

46553CB00005B/2195